JUDGMENT DAY

Judgment Day

COLEEN LIEBSCH
Laszlo Kugler

Performance Strategies Publishing

JUDGMENT DAY
By Coleen Liebsch
Copyright 2020 Performance Strategies Publishing

Cover Art by Laszlo Kugler
Editing by Deborah Merkwan
All rights reserved. Printed in the USA. No part of this book may be reproduced or copied in any form without express written permission from the publisher.
ISBN: 978-1-942333-23-4
10 9 8 7 6 5 4 3 2

Judgment Day

I'm not sure when I realized I was dead. I remember thinking "I can't survive this..." as a huge ball of fire raced toward me down the narrow tunnel of road. It was consuming my options before my brain could even comprehend what was happening. What in the... How can I... Then everything went black. Did the world end? What could have caused something like that? And suddenly none of my questions mattered.

My day began as normally as any other day. I woke up early figuring I would be able to get a jump on the day. My family, however, decided to be particularly needy, so the extra time I had was taken up with last minute homework help, mismatched clothing dilemmas and sack lunches because the lunch at school was unacceptable to my finicky children. What SHOULD have started out as a day of extra time for ME, wound up being about everyone else instead. I remember thinking how sick I am of raising teenagers.

My oldest daughter is 16 and believes the world revolves around her every move. Just last night she was ranting and raving about how the mothers of her friends were way better than I was and how she wished she could have been born in THEIR family rather than mine. I certainly couldn't argue with her about that. I was wishing the exact same thing myself.

My youngest child was even worse. She turned herself off about a year ago and uses any time she has at home as an exercise in isolation. All she ever does is sit in her room with her stereo blaring. When she DOES come downstairs with the rest of us she just mopes around and mumbles whatever it is she is thinking. Generally speaking it's something awful about me. Half of the time I want to pretend I don't even know her when we're in public.

Her clothing choices are an embarrassment to the family, and if she comes home with another piercing, she can just find somewhere else to live! How could God have given me such awful children when all I ever wanted was to be a good mom?

It might help if their father was ever around. I realize that he works hard at his job, but so do I! The difference is that after I get off work I have to hurry home to start cooking a dinner that no one will appreciate. After he finishes with work, he volunteers for the church or the legion. How is any of THAT helping our family? It isn't even like the people he's volunteering to help appreciate him! I can't believe I married someone as selfish as he is!

The only good thing about him anymore is his paycheck, and even THAT isn't enough most of the time. As I thought back through my day and the ingrates I lived with, I realized that maybe I was glad to be dead.

The dark seems to be changing to a glow, but there doesn't seem to be a source for the light. It is simply everywhere. My eyes haven't completely adjusted, but it's bright now. It's not just bright, it's getting brighter, and I can't close my eyes or look away from it. It is getting so bright that it's going to burn my eyes out in a second. So why aren't my eyes starting to hurt? Why is it that NOTHING actually hurts? Between my arthritis and knee problems, I haven't had a day without pain in decades, until now.

I don't miss anyone. I don't look forward to anything. I quite simply, exist. As my vision adjusts to the bright lights, I begin to see definitions. They're vague at first, like clouds, but then they begin to take form.

I start to make out beautiful architecture leading up to a grand castle far off in the distance. It reminds me of the castle at Magic Kingdom and fills me with excitement. I see manicured landscapes and topiary gardens that are more beautifully perfect than anything I've ever seen, even in magazines!

The foliage is perfect and provides a stupendous foreground to rolling hills under brilliant skies. There are statues and fountains creating an unparalleled elegance far grander than the greatest cathedral!

As I get closer to them, I realize that nothing I thought I was seeing was real. They are being formed by flocks of angels arranged in a way they believe will be a pleasing view for me. Millions of wings are outstretched as the angels watch me anxiously, waiting for me to comprehend what I am seeing.

At that moment I begin to hear a faint melody. It starts almost like a memory or a soft, subtle background noise. It becomes louder, but the notes are nothing that I recognize. It is as if my ears have never heard music, and I become enthralled with the melody. The voices of a million angels blend perfectly in a wordless chorus that has no end. Even without words the message is unquestionably one of peace and love.

Just like with the brilliant light, the music fills me completely, and I know that even if I listen to it for a thousand years it would never become routine. My human ears could never have heard or appreciated the sounds as they trilled and floated together in utter perfection.

As I realize where I am, I accept it with no uncertainty. I am dead.

The angels began to move, as if in synch with the music, to create a path. Their flowing gowns of unblemished white clouds swirled and danced with every movement. Their knowing eyes and harmonic voices follow me as I walk the path created by their multitudes. Their joy and overwhelming love doesn't just flow through me, it fills me.

It is all so beautiful and peaceful as I melted into the perfection. I no longer worried about anything worldly and had to remind myself that it had even existed.

I remembered my loved ones fondly, but so many foreign things joined them in my heart. It was not unlike getting used to the bright light. My heart was so full of love that surely there couldn't be another drop of happiness added. And yet, instead of exploding, my heart was unconfined by humanity. It was infinite. God had called me home, and I was ready to spend eternity in heaven.

As the path narrowed towards the horizon of angels, I noticed a figure standing in the middle of the path. I know instantly who He is, even from that great distance. My heart again felt it would explode with joy.

I was on the path that would lead me to Jesus!

I tried to hurry my pace, but no longer remembered how to run or swim or propel myself in any way. I simply floated peacefully along the path, knowing that Jesus was waiting for me ahead.

I began to understand the things that had eluded me in life. I thought I knew the color white. In life it was the color that most obsessed my life. There was the laundry that would never get clean enough. I thought of my counters that were forever stained because no one else seemed to understand how to clean them.

I remembered the appliances and bathroom fixtures. How many hours had I spent scrubbing them to reach the color that I believed to be pure white? Without the obstruction of my human eyes, I saw the color for what it really was: an extravagant collection of every color imaginable and hundreds more that I could never have imagined. Every tint, every nuance was crystal clear and I found myself getting lost in the beauty before me. I had no idea that as I was admiring the beauty surrounding me I was also moving closer to Jesus.

When I reached the Lord Jesus, I was again astounded at what I never would have noticed in life. His outstretched arms received me, and I knew immediately I was home. I remembered my life and realized how often I had longed for someone to hold me and make everything alright. How long had I cared for others while wishing that someone would care for me? Had I felt this way as a child? I couldn't remember a time when I felt so completely filled with peace and comfort.

As Jesus held me in his arms, he absorbed every worry, every resentment, and every grudge I had ever carried in life.

I looked up to see that his face was far more glorious than I ever would have imagined. His spirit glowed with the power of the Holy Spirit.

I was home.

I have no perception of how long I've rested in Jesus' arms. It could be a day, it could be a millennium. It didn't matter; I would never grow accustomed to the perfection or wish for a change. But then suddenly, change is exactly what happened.

When I looked up to view my Lord's face again, I saw that He was crying.

My confusion was total. Wasn't this a good thing? I was finally getting to heaven and it was even better than I ever imagined!

Without any warning, a horrible chorus of trumpets blared across the fields of angels, and a booming voice from above called out a name that was completely foreign to me.

Without any awareness of change, I was suddenly walking on what appeared to be clouds. I felt the sensation of holding Jesus' hand as he led me toward something, but the clouds were obstructing my view.

The fog cleared slowly to reveal the end of the path.

Although everything had changed as completely as possible, it all looked the same. The angels sang the same beautiful songs, but they were no longer the focus of my existence.

I knew where I stood.

I was standing at the foot of the grandest throne to ever exist. More beautiful than gold and diamonds, more majestic than any castle ever created, but suddenly I felt cold. It was as if I had a body that was standing inside a cold, stone castle, and my feelings of eternal peace were fading.

It was Jesus that addressed God but the words he spoke were not in a language I'd heard before.

I watched their brief exchange like I watched my parents as a child. And just like back then, the attention turned back to me all too soon. There are no human words to describe God's voice and no language known on earth that expresses the words. It is as if every cell in my body received the message at the exact same moment even though no words were spoken. I knew that my moment of judgment had arrived.

The trumpets sounded again and I realized they weren't trumpets at all. The sound was like a combination of a fog horn, conch shells and a ship blaring. It was ghastly in contrast to the rest of my surroundings and the sound did not fill my soul with a feeling of comfort or reassurance. It was filling me with a feeling of doom, and I struggled to think back on my life.

It already seemed so distant it was hard to even pinpoint one specific memory, much less reflect on all my sins. But I remembered something about how it didn't matter. All I needed to do was believe in Jesus Christ and my salvation was guaranteed.

I had gone to church almost every Sunday of my life and I never broke any of the major commandments. Why did I feel so exposed and vulnerable? Why did I wish I were able to run away?

Suddenly images flashed through my mind more quickly than I would have thought imaginable. And yet I was able to follow each event as if it were being played in slow motion.

I saw myself as a little girl, a teenager, a young bride and a young mother. I watched as the years flew by. My body aged and my resentments compounded. Surely God would know it wasn't MY fault that my life had been filled with such hateful people.

As each memory replayed I had a new awareness of what my actions or lack of actions meant. For the first time, I saw how my life affected those around me.

Jesus stood firmly by my side with tears rolling down his cheeks as each event replayed from a new point of view. No matter how quickly the events passed, my thoughts had no problem keeping up.

While each event replayed and each outcome was exposed, God's judgment was passed. I didn't need to hear the words "guilty", "guilty", "guilty" to know God's judgment. I clearly felt each one.

Like the time I committed murder. I held no weapon against another human being while I was alive but I committed murder just the same. I watched the replay of an event that was no more significant in my life than a day of rain at the time it was happening.

I was running a daycare while my children were young to bring in some extra money without having to work outside my home. I had several competitors in town that I didn't feel were a good influence on children. It wasn't just my opinion either, most of my friends felt the exact same way. The one at the end of my block was the worst, but most of the parents who hired the lady weren't much better themselves.

On the day in question, a child under her care wandered into my yard while I was outside with the kids I watched. I looked at the child, wearing nothing but a diaper, and I remember thinking what a ridiculous excuse of a daycare provider I had for competition. I remember feeling a little satisfied that something like that would never happen on my watch but certainly God couldn't find fault with ME about that! I remember taking the children I was paid to watch back inside my house. They didn't need to see the filthy little boy any more than I needed to see him.

A few hours later parents started picking up their children when I heard the sirens of an ambulance approaching. We peered down the street and noticed the crowd gathered around something in the road and the urgency of the ambulance was obvious. I remarked to the parents that it wasn't any wonder one of the kids she watched had been hurt. I told them about the one little boy that had been wandering around my yard most of the morning and they AGREED with my disgust. It wasn't me! It was the daycare lady down the street!

God's wordless reply came through every cell in my body. "I put you there to save the life of one of my children. When you turned your back on him, you turned your back on me."

"But God," I pleaded, "I didn't know what would happen. He wasn't my responsibility! How could I have known that?"

But even before God's wordless response, I knew that I should have known. A child that age, wandering around alone, was obviously at a high risk of injury. God knew my heart better than I did and I couldn't even lie to myself anymore.

I watched myself as a young child in grade school. One of my classmates was a boy who I knew nothing about except his name. He almost always needed a bath and smelled bad whenever I got close, so I tried my best to avoid him. For some reason though, he seemed to like me better than the other kids and he was always trying to be my friend. I could never figure out what made him think I could ever be interested in someone like him but apparently, he did.

Every day he brought something to school to show to me or give to me. I never asked him for anything or accepted anything from him, so it wasn't MY fault he was kidding himself into believing we were friends! Besides that, why wouldn't it be HIS fault for trying to buy my friendship like that?

I was never the first one to START any of the awful things we said and did to him. All I ever tried to do was avoid him! It wasn't my fault! I know that he was always nice to me, but does that mean I had to like him back? I didn't stand up for him because they would have all turned on ME! I couldn't defend him and keep my friends. The only thing it would have accomplished is getting BOTH of us picked on. He wasn't my responsibility!

Suddenly I was filled with empathy and knowledge and I saw for the first time what his life had been. He had moved to our town to live with an aunt after his parents were killed in a car accident. His aunt had tremendous resentment toward the boy who lived through an event that took her beloved sister, and she took every opportunity to punish him for it.

I never saw the bruises on his body, so how was I supposed to know he was abused? How was I to know that he snarfed down his food like a pig at lunch because he hadn't eaten since his last meal at the school? How would I have known that he lived his life in the root cellar of his aunt's home because she was too disgusted with him to allow him in her house? I was just a kid! What was I supposed to do?

The silent realization passed through me as I understood that God did wasn't judging me for doing the wrong thing. He was judging me for doing nothing.

I saw myself as a teenager. So many of my decisions were made based on what I thought people wanted to hear. But even so, I wasn't the only one who talked behind people's backs!

I grew up in a small town, EVERYONE was that way! I watched as one of the girls in my class sat with her head down, away from the rest of us. I had barely noticed her at the time, but when I did see her she just seemed like a freak. She never spoke. She always wore black clothes and a trench coat, so I never had the chance to even SEE that her arms were covered in scars from cutting herself. It wasn't like she ever asked me for help or anything!

God have mercy, I didn't know any better. But again, I knew that was a lie before my mind even finished the thought. Guilty!

"Dear God, please show mercy on my soul!" I turned to Jesus who looked at me with a profound sadness beyond any imagination. "Please, Lord Jesus, you were human once. Please tell Him that I'm only human! I know not what I do right? You know how hard it is to live every single second of the day worrying about every single thing you do! Please, Jesus, Please! Tell Him that I tried! I went to church almost every Sunday, I took communion just a few days before I died, I'm not one of those low life's who spent their life in a bar! I volunteered for the church ALL THE TIME! Doesn't that count for anything?!?"

As if on cue, scenes from my life at church began flashing before me. I recalled the baptism of a baby born out of wedlock. The reason I didn't look at the baby when the minister presented it to the church is because it was a bastard! The bible clearly says that pre-marital sex is wrong yet here stands a woman, by herself because she couldn't even keep the baby's father in her life, who was not only a sinner but proud enough of her sin to baptize the kid in front of our whole congregation. If she was going to have it baptized, the least she could have done was to have the ceremony in private!

That wasn't MY sin! It was hers and also the minister's for allowing something like that to even happen in a house of God.

I knew, of course, that my own pre-marital promiscuities were already known to God, but it was not like I was dumb enough to get pregnant! Once again I was shown visions of scenes I knew nothing about in life.

I watched as the young girl left the nightclub where she worked as a waitress. She worked evenings to put herself through school during the day. I felt her fear as she neared an entrance to a dark alley, she passed every single night. A feeling of foreboding increased. I saw the man crouching behind the dumpster until she had almost made it past the alley entrance. I saw him jump out and grab her.

I felt her panic as she struggled to pull his hand from her face, not just to scream but to breath. I felt the pain as his fist met her jaw before he threw her to the ground behind the dumpster.

I realized she was lying on shards of broken beer bottles and gravel from the road before the first piece began to tear at her skin. I felt the cold as he ripped her coat and clothing away from her body with one hand and held a knife to her throat with the other. I felt the warmth of her tears as they ran down her cheek mixing with blood and dirt as they fell. I felt her fear but could barely comprehend its origin.

The young woman's fear revolved around what would become of her invalid mother if she didn't return home to care for her. I felt her revulsion as the monster took her innocence with some kind of a pipe before violating her himself. I understood her longing to die as her attacker kicked her in the head one last time before leaving her for dead in the dark alley.

I watched as she found the strength to pull herself up and stumble out of the alley to try to find help. I saw the people on the sidewalk cross the street to avoid the responsibility of getting involved and I felt each new injury as she fell again and again. I watched as she finally entered the hospital bleeding and disoriented, collapsing in the entry way. I saw the police interrogate her about what had happened while the doctors still worked on her body. I heard the officers ask about her clothing and whether she made a practice of wearing such provocative outfits.

Time must have passed, because I saw her bruises fading to green and yellow and her cuts becoming thin lines of scars around her face. I saw her sitting in the doctor's office when he gave her the news that she was pregnant, and I felt her pain as she wept into her hands.

I saw her alone in the delivery room as she gave birth to a beautiful baby girl not unlike my own daughters. I heard her prayers for strength to accomplish the tremendously difficult task set before her of raising a child born out of violence. I felt her heart as she first looked into eyes that were just like her own.

For the first time, I felt love that had no conditions or history. I heard her first conversation with her child when she told the tiny baby HOW she came into the world meant nothing. The fact that she DID come into the world meant everything.

Just as quickly as my own life passed before my eyes, hers replayed.

I saw her working two jobs to put herself through school while still paying for the care of her daughter and mother. I felt the love in her heart each time she kissed her mother's forehead before bed and I felt her heartache at her mother's passing.

The young woman felt no relief at the lifting of one of her burdens. The only relief she felt was that her mother's suffering had come to an end.

I watched her straighten her little girl's dress as she prepared to let her go to her first day of pre-school. Again, she felt no relief over the lessoning of her burdens. She felt only pride and love for the little girl that had filled her memories with love and laughter.

I watched her chew her nails at work as she worried that her baby wouldn't eat enough at lunch. I watched her glance at the clock repeatedly as she patiently bodes time's passing.

I watched her grab her purse and run for the elevator when it was time to pick up her daughter. I saw her tapping her toes outside of the pre-school room as she worried about whether the other children had been kind to her baby, and if the teacher understood what a treasure she was.

Although no one else noticed, I saw her quickly brush a tear of relief away as her daughter bounced into her arms with stories about the joys of pre-school. I felt her joy as her daughter recounted every moment of the day and was amazed at the mother's ability to ward off boredom, even over the most trivial of details.

I saw her repeatedly refuse offers to brighten her own social life to be a part of every moment with her daughter.

I felt her pride when the daughter moved her tassel from one side of the graduation cap to the other, symbolizing her step into adult hood. Even now I couldn't comprehend the utter lack of relief she felt. The woman was sad that her biggest chore would be coming to an end. I knew those were not the feelings I would have in her shoes.

Jesus wept in silence.

I felt the change in my heart first, but it was only a fraction of a second before the rest of my soul felt it too.

For the first time in my existence there was an emptiness so profoundly complete there could be only one cause.

God's judgment was passed, and He was gone. Not just from my vision, He was gone from my soul. In His place, nothing remained but an eternal emptiness. A black hole that clawed and grabbed everything favorable from my memories. All it left behind was emptiness.

God had given up on me, and I was damned. The horrible trumpets that sounded like a combination of fog horns and off key brass instruments blared.

Jesus took my hand as He turned to walk me back down the path of angels. It was the exact same path I had just crossed with joyful exuberance. The path that had led me to the light of existence was now intending to lead me into a dark pit. The harmonic voices of the angels were silenced and the only sound in their place was the occasional splash of a tear as it landed on the stone path.

But Jesus was still with me and that had to mean there was hope. Surely I could convince him to at least TALK to God on my behalf. He knew my questions before they were asked, and I realized I was not the first person He had walked back down the path.

How many others were there who didn't know they were committing sins against God? How many others didn't know their selfishness was damning them! How many others were lying to themselves? Someone needs to warn them at least!

Finally, Jesus spoke.

"My Father gave His laws, written in stone, to the multitudes, and it wasn't enough. He sent the Holy Spirit to fill each soul with empathy and remain in each person as their conscience. It wasn't enough. He asked my Mother to watch as the soldiers flailed and whipped me beyond recognition, and it wasn't enough. He sent me to show the multitudes that the trials of life are worth ANY price, and yet it wasn't enough.

When my death failed to make the multitudes rise up against the tyranny of mob rule, He told me that it was enough. There were no other sacrifices that could be made, no other lessons that would have demonstrated the point more clearly, and yet, it has never been enough.

I BEGGED my Father to forgive you and pleaded that you just didn't know what you were doing but your heart is transparent to our Father. He knows that you've heard the lessons and you've said the prayers. You felt the pain and yet rejoiced at the suffering of others. You may have hidden that joy from the world, and you may have hidden your judgment from your neighbors, but NOTHING is hidden from God.

I have BEGGED my Father for centuries to allow me to defend my brothers and sisters on their day of judgment and because His love is never ending, He has allowed me that privilege. And still, I am left with nothing to defend you."

Surely He had to be wrong. I might not have been the best person in the world, but I certainly wasn't the worst either.

I pleaded in vain.

"But I haven't actually killed anyone or stolen anything even close to the amount that has been stolen from me! I haven't cheated on my husband, even though I COULD have on several different occasions! I spent my whole life minding my own business and even if I DID do some things wrong, at least it wasn't as bad as the child murderers or the prostitutes!"

I knew I was ranting but my desperation increased with each step we took. "For crying out loud, even the bible talks about how you defended a prostitute. You could do that and still not defend me after all the times I've prayed to you?"

With my words, Jesus lowered his head and stopped walking. He turned toward me and said "You still don't get it do you? It isn't about anyone else. This is YOUR judgment day and our Father doesn't grade on a curve. This is about what you did and didn't do with the talents and opportunities you were given. He gave you the ability to notice tiny details so you could see His children's needs more clearly than others. You used it to judge someone's shoes. He gave you the means to be able to support your family and still have money left over. Yet you refused to share those gifts with someone who needed them more." I knew even before he spoke them that the words were all true. I also knew that His list wasn't finished. "God gave you more than you needed then put you in the path of some of His children who needed help. Remember the homeless man outside of Wal-Mart? God sent you there to help one of his children and you not only refused to share what God had provided, you mocked a child of God as you walked by. "

He continued. "You knew how it felt to be the new person in town, so God put you on the path towards one of His children who was going through the exact same thing. You could have made her feel welcome but instead you pointed out the groups she wasn't likely to qualify for. Did you even know they moved three months later and had to sell almost everything they owned in order to do so?

God gave you the ability to speak and walk so that you could HELP your fellow man. How did you use those gifts? You used them to put people down. You used them to HURT other children of God. You believe if your hand didn't deal the blow you are innocent of abuse. You've believed that you could somehow win the favor of God by pointing out the flaws of His other children."

My emotions were torn. I wanted Jesus to stop reminding me about my life, yet I wanted Him to talk forever so we wouldn't have to walk further down the path to the darkness. He went on.

"God gave you children so you could understand His love for you. You professed your love for your children when their behavior pleased you and withheld your love when it didn't. Fear of your judgment prevented your son from ever admitting to himself he was homosexual. Fear of your judgment caused him to take his own life. You wanted to believe you spent the rest of your life mourning his death. What you actually did was steal the tragedy of his life to prolong sympathy and attention for yourself. You have hidden your shame about his lifestyle by perpetuating the lies that simply made YOU feel and look better. You worried more about appearances than you did about God's law! You quoted the bible as you passed your judgments and assumed that meant you were speaking for God!"

I could feel the end approaching, but he continued. "The Bible is a collection of stories from people who weren't afraid to talk about their relationships with God... people who weren't afraid to talk about their relationship with ME! It wasn't supposed to end! God gave you and all of mankind free will. It was up to YOU to choose how to use it. It was up to YOU to choose your path. You ignored God's inspiration and guidance even at the end when He put the path he wanted you to take right in front of you! And still you ignored Him! How can you ask me to defend the defenseless? How can you ask me, who accepted EVERY path my father laid before me to defend you, who accepted none? You were put in a position of affluence to stand up for those who weren't and instead you mocked them. You ask me to defend you because you put money in an offering plate? You heard the scripture about false gods and yet you valued your coin and the work that IT could do above the works of our Father. You had the privilege to hear exactly what you needed to do and still you ignored God's will."

I knew He was right.

I was defenseless.

"I did not die on the cross to give you free reign without consequences. I died to show you that no sacrifice is too great and no path is too treacherous. I died to show you that it was worth any torture on earth to have God's favor in eternity. You cannot claim ignorance after knowing the truth. I have wasted my time and love believing in you, hoping you would see the light. But today you have broken my heart for the last time. From this moment forward you will walk your path alone. Stripped of any relationship with me and stripped of your memories from life."

I was afraid to look up because I already knew in my heart Jesus was gone. The emptiness in my heart began to spread as I tried to hold onto memories of my children, my husband, my parents, my family, and my friends. But one by one the emptiness overtook them.

I am standing on a path that has only one direction. I do not want to move forward but I don't really know why. It's dark and I don't think I like dark. I'm not going to move so it doesn't matter what lies at the end. I thought maybe I'd just lie down for a while and sleep some of this off but when I look down at the path I see that it is moving. I look up and realize that the dark is getting closer. I want to close my eyes but I can't. I try to look away, but I can't. I can no longer deny that the dark is creeping toward me.

Different shades of black swirl together in a serpentine fashion on both sides of the path. As the dark approaches I begin to see more details and realize that the tubular beings that were winding and slithering around, above and on the path I was quickly approaching. What I thought were snakes were large formations of lost souls moving in synchronized patterns that made them look like snakes.

As the path brought them closer, I began to see their faces. The frozen looks of terror and anger drew their faces out into long ghoulish masks of torture. Their bodies were nothing more than a flowing collection of smoke that moved in conjunction with their masks. Maybe I am going somewhere different than they are because I still had legs!

I looked down at my legs only to realize that they had already been replaced by the flowing gown of nothing. I was too close and I couldn't move! The shadows wound around me, beside me, through me, and as each lost soul intersected with me I gained their pain as well as my own. I started to scream but there was no sound. I could feel my face stretching out into my own mask of torture. I turned to go back the other way only to find that the path had disappeared.

I was now moving in synch with a tubular group swirling through me, filling me with their horrors and taking on mine. Was there something before this? Are we going somewhere?

I try to look around, but every view is filled with more lost souls. They aren't just travelling through me, they are eating me!

The fights begin as each lost soul tries to take a piece of my humanity. I am defenseless against so many but surely it can't last long! Is there anything left for them to take from me?

I cry out in pain, but my sound is lost as it mixes with the multitudes of screams around me.

How long has this been going on?

How much longer will it last?

How can there be anything left of me for them to eat away?

A soul! A new soul is entering somewhere. I must have it! I'm trying frantically to push my way through the tentacles of formations but I cannot leave my group. I can smell the new soul and I want it! Why can't I move through my formation? I am being held in place by the souls that are feasting on me and I cannot break free. I scream in torture but it wasn't even loud enough for ME to hear it. I am lost in a sea of hatred. I am bathed in an ocean of pain. I remember that water used to mean something and I become thirsty. I am so thirsty!

Have I ever tasted water?

Is there anything here that could quench my thirst?

I feel my mouth crack from the lack of moisture but as I look around me at the masks of horror, I see that their mouths and faces are cracked with dehydration as well.

There is no relief. There will never again BE relief.

With that realization I begin the scream that will never end.